The Lost Coin
Finding the Missing Piece

Sharifa Stirgus

DEDICATION

To the women who were taken advantage of at an early age, who struggle from an identity crisis due to past trauma or manipulation...

To those who have lost a loved one and seek refuge in others to replace a void only God can fill...

To those who try to accomplish goals in your own strength...

To the many who've gone in the wrong direction looking for a sense of belonging...

To those who feel the need to compromise to be validated and loved...

We choose to speak to you because we all know what it feels like to be broken, hurt and abandoned. Although you may think you've lost the most precious things in this world, we want to encourage you they can be found by searching deep within yourself and with the love of God.

You are an Overcomer! You are Wanted! You are Needed!

This book is dedicated to you.

CONTENTS

ACKNOWLEDGMENTS

First, I give honor and thanks to God for giving me the vision for this book project and the opportunity to put it into action. Secondly, I thank all the amazing people who have helped me along the way.

Words alone are not enough to express my true gratitude for my husband, Shon, and his emotional support and encouragement to keep moving forward in creating this book. Thank you so much!

To my beautiful daughters, Alayah and Jayla, for understanding my long nights at the kitchen table writing, I truly thank you!

To my Writing Coach & Editor, Kocysha LaShaun, who helped all of us in so many ways, thank you. I deeply appreciate your patience, executive advice, and self-publishing assistance. May you continue to do what God has called you to do. Thank you sincerely!

To my Book Cover/Graphic Designer, Crystal Hairston, thank you for your patience, enthusiasm, and your amazing creativity. May God continue to bless you in all that you do! Thank you!

To my amazing Co-authors, Ronnetta Rockamore, Karena Washington, Tatiana Glass, and Kocysha LaShaun, thank each of you for accepting the invite to be a part of this anthology project without hesitation. Thanks for all of your time, energy, and words of encouragement. I could not have done this without you. May you all continue to be awesome authors with the Grace of God upon your lives! Thank you!

To my god-sister and counselor, Amber Broadway, I thank you for our long talks and advice given to help me through a very emotional part in my life while writing my stories. May you be blessed will all God has for you. Thank you kindly!

To First Lady Jacqueline Y. Stewart, my spiritual mother, thank you for being the leader that you are. Thanks for encouraging me to go out and pursue my God-given goals. I'm so grateful. May you and your family be blessed and highly favored. Thank you!

FOREWORD

I have been impressed with the drive, talent, motivation as well as the uniqueness of Sharifa Stirgus ever since she joined ACTS Ministries. As the pastor's wife and First Lady, Sharifa and I have sat down and had awesome talks and dialogue as spiritual mother and daughter. We have discussed subjects regarding ministry, writing, goals and so many other exciting topics of interest. In the story of *The Lost Coin*, Sharifa and the co-authors candidly share their heartfelt and compelling testimonies that are sure to ignite your thinking and bless you in the process.

This book is an eye-opening revelation that will cause you to step back and take another investigative look at your own life. Yes, we all have lost exquisite, dear, rare, precious and valuable coins, even if it took us a while to realize the coin was actually lost. Maybe it was something tangible like a car, a house, a job or a position. Perhaps it was something as priceless as a friendship, a loved one, a spouse, or yourself!

I am moved at the honesty, openness and vulnerability of the writers as they share great losses in their own lives and how they were able, with God's help, to find and restore the very things which they had lost. Being full, satisfied, complete and whole is something we all yearn for with nothing missing and nothing lost. When we discover that something or a piece to the culmination of who we are is missing, we must seek out deliberately and diligently how, when, where and why we lost it in order to receive complete restoration.

Several chapters resonated with me as Sharifa shared her vision with me and as she and the other ladies tell their compelling stories. You will enjoy taking the unparalleled journey to finding your *Lost Coin* as each writer elaborates on, and shares some rare, but important coins that were lost in their own lives.

With over thirty-five years of ministry and encountering people from all walks of life, I believe that this book will help close some unwanted doors, and open up fresh new windows of opportunities to help you attain the fullness and completion God designed for you. The story of *The Lost Coin* not only magnifies and helps you to see what you've lost but also sheds light on how to find it with valuable lessons learned and uplifting words of encouragement shared! May you experience God's healing presence as you personally receive the message of *The Lost Coin: Finding the Missing Piece*!

Jacqueline Y. Stewart
ACTS Ministries First Lady

Epigraph

"Or what woman, having ten silver coins, if she loses one coin, does not light a lamp, sweep the house and search carefully until she finds *it?*

And when she has found *it,* she calls *her* friends and neighbors together, saying, 'Rejoice with me, for I have found the piece which I lost!'"

~Luke 15:8-9 NKJV~

Being Held Accountable

"So then every one of us shall give account of himself to God."
~Romans 14:12, KJV~

There's nothing like a sense of freedom. Free as a bird, traveling through life on your own terms – having no worries. Sounds rejuvenating and refreshing, right? What if that freedom left you feeling invincible. Mid 2009 I was without accountability and I truly felt invincible.

Losing a parent can damage one in ways you could never imagine. I lost my parents almost a year apart: June 29, 2008 (mom) and June 24, 2009 (dad). It wasn't just the loss of both parents that affected me, it was also the loss of accountability. Growing up my parents weren't married, nor did we all live under the same roof, but there was always consistent expectations and accountability from both of them. Their spoken expectations were to finish school and make a successful and productive life for yourself. There was also an unspoken expectation, I felt, that sort of stemmed from who they were. I felt responsible to carry myself a certain way in public because I was Dene and Butch's daughter. Growing up in a small town, everyone knew you and your parents. Any public slip up and you better believe your parents would know about it in the snap of a finger. As a teenager, I had my fun, but I made sure it was in a way my parents wouldn't be made aware. I didn't want to disappoint them.

Fast forward to the summer of 2009. The two people I'd lived to please and not disappoint had been taken away. In my mind I'm thinking gloves off because there is no one left on this earth to hold me accountable. There's no one left that I wanted to please. I knew God was watching, but I could easily ignore that thought because it's not like He was going to pick up the phone to call and check on me. Therefore, I didn't have to worry about explaining my actions to Him. What I didn't realize was the dark and lonely place I was about to enter due to that mindset. I was 27, single, living in the city, and no one to question my actions. Let the undisciplined living begin! I became reckless in my decision-making concerning relationships. Discernment was out the door. I began mingling with men who I knew my parents, especially my mom, would not approve of, but I didn't have to answer to them anymore. For a moment in time, all of their talks and advice were null and void. I went through weeks of dating several men. None of them actually gave me what I was looking for or thought I needed, so I constantly switched up. I wasn't necessarily wanting a relationship. I was okay living this free life even if it went against everything that had been instilled in me. What I learned, however, is that it wasn't free; it was costing me a heavy price. It was costing me myself.

My mom passed away after a six-month battle with cancer. I was angry at her for leaving us. She was diagnosed with cancer December 2007. They began chemo treatment immediately. After months of trying various treatments, her doctor told her he had no other options. He offered to refer her to a cancer doctor in Texas, but she refused. She said she was tired and in too much pain for that type of travel. I accepted her decision at the moment because it was her decision to make. Honestly, I couldn't see cancer taking her out. After she passed away, I didn't understand why she chose to stop fighting. She had been fighting for her girls all of our lives, always putting us before herself. Why stop now when she was needed the most? I was angry at her for not doing what she had done since I could remember: fighting to be there and make sure we were okay. So this built up anger, coupled with no accountability made it easy to live my life as I chose, regardless of the consequences. I felt justified in the decisions I was making. It was as if I wanted to get back at her for leaving us. I understood later that my mom's purpose here on this earth had been fulfilled. She didn't give up; God called her home.

Back to the summer of 2009, I was also losing the voice of the Holy Spirit. It wasn't like the Holy Spirit or God left me, but I had definitely pushed them away. I didn't care about being held accountable by the very entity that saw fit to take my parents away. I did everything humanly possible to block them out of my life. I was answering to no one but myself.

I'll never forget one evening as I sat on my sofa – with

just the light from my lamps beaming off of the walls – I began bawling my eyes out (you know that ugly cry), until I had the most excruciating headache. I began pleading with God for His forgiveness. I had reached an emotional breaking point. I didn't recognize myself anymore. I no longer knew what I did or did not stand for, but I knew God was the only one that could save me from myself.

God is a jealous God. We are commanded to honor our mother and father but not worship them to the point where their opinion matters more than God's. Holding myself accountable to God's expectations should have been priority first and foremost. Had that been in place, I would not have felt so free to live as I pleased, which ended, by the way, with me begging and pleading to God for forgiveness (and a cross tattoo).

Living a life without accountability may initially seem rejuvenating, but our actions that follow will leave us feeling anything but rejuvenated. The Holy Spirit is our guiding voice. Holding ourselves accountable to God's expectations is what will keep us grounded and consistent. When we shift our thinking and we put people in God's place, it can leave us unsettled when those people are removed from our lives. People are going to come in and out of our lives, but God's presence is constant. God has to be our source of accountability. Our true peace and solid foundation lies in our ability to hold ourselves accountable to His standards.

Encouraged to Empower

As I began my journey back to holding myself accountable to God's expectations, there were several steps I took into account. For me, I knew these steps were not only important but necessary.

1. **Reconnect with God.** It's difficult to hold yourself accountable to someone with whom you have no connection. Take time to search Bible plans on accountability that speak to you.

   Where do you see a need to reconnect with God? How can this be implemented?

   _____

   _____

   _____

   _____

2. **Step away.** Give yourself time every day to reconnect with God. Make a schedule and decide if this time will take place in the morning before your day begins or in

the evening. Start small, if you need to, with 5-10 minutes of uninterrupted time with God.

What time do you believe best to spend time with God? How many minutes will you begin with?

_____

_____

3. **Find an accountability partner.** Find 1-2 spiritually grounded individuals who will strongly encourage you on a daily basis to remain connected to God and His expectations for you and your life.

List names of individuals who you can trust to be a reliable accountability partner? If no one, how can you hold yourself accountable in ways you haven't before?

_____

_____

_____

_____

Staying grounded in the Word and in the presence of God is truly your saving grace. I know that may sound cliché-ish because you hear it so often, but it is truly your foundation, your blueprint of life. Be honest with yourself about whose expectations you're living up to. Is it God's, or the people in your life? If you're not holding yourself accountable to God's expectations, you'll have to shift your thinking.

Ask yourself the question, 'Who am I most concerned about disappointing?' If your answer is not God, then His expectations of you will not be a priority in your life. There will come a time when you will have to pause and check back in with God. There will be a little nudging in your spirit. That nudging is the Holy Spirit letting you know that you have gotten off course.

Pray with Me

Heavenly Father, Your Word, the Holy Bible, is my guide and source of accountability. Thank You for providing me with not only Your Word, but with the Holy Spirit to help me on my journey. I live to bring glory and honor to the Kingdom of God. Thank You for Your unfailing love.

The lost coin of accountability has now been found.
Let us rejoice in the name of Jesus. Amen.

Finding the Right Fit

"Therefore confess your sins to each other and pray for each other so that you may be healed. The prayer of a righteous person is powerful and effective."
~James 5:16, NIV~

"Call it a network, call it a tribe, call it a family; whatever you call it, whoever you are, you need one." (Jane Howard) After the death of my parents, I went through a phase of exploring the freedom of not living up to their expectations and then I entered a phase of feeling like I didn't belong. I didn't feel connected to a family unit. Maslow's Hierarchy references the importance of feeling love and belonging. It's difficult to explain, but something shifts inside of you when you lose your parents. Even though I still had a good relationship with some members of my family, there was still something missing – the two people that birthed me into the family. Without them it felt like my rooted connections to a family unit were demolished. Until I met a guy…

Not only did he come with a father and stepmother but also a sister and a niece. It may not have been the perfect family, but nonetheless it was a family. After losing

14

my parents and moving to a city where I didn't know anyone, this was the perfect way to put those pieces back together. At least that's what I thought. Sometimes in life we can become so mentally and emotionally unregulated we only focus on what we have lost. In doing so we try to figure out ways, on our own, to replace something without consulting God.

I was eager to jump into this relationship because I felt like it would fill that void of needing to belong. I had a companion and a new family. I wish I could say there was a happily ever after ending to this, but the next two and a half years were nothing but turmoil. When we first met, I was living by myself, in school, and working. I was living a pretty simple and quiet life. Six months later, he was in rehab for drugs and I was wondering what the heck had I gotten myself into. Little did I know the uncharted path I was about to walk. When he got out of rehab, he revealed that he went in because he was a heroin user. Y'all I didn't even know what heroin was or the seriousness of this drug, but ba-by I was about to find out!

I have this nurturing complex, which sometimes can be a curse. When he got out of rehab and made this revelation, I was like, "Okay let's keep moving forward. We can beat this together!" I wasn't ready to walk away from this relationship, even though it had become mentally and emotionally exhausting because of the need to belong.

Things began to get worse. At first it was like $5 or $10 here and there that he would take out of my purse. We would talk about it, he would cry and profoundly profess his deepest apologies. I would forgive him, and we would let bygones be bygones. Then the small bills turned into bigger bills. There was one situation where I noticed I was missing $100 that was part of my rent money. I'm pretty meticulous about any cash I carry so I knew that I hadn't lost the money. My mind immediately went to him, but I was like there's no way he's taken $100 from me – not with all that we've been through and how much I've been there for him. There's no way! Well, yes he did! He admitted to it and tried to downplay the situation by saying that he would pay me back and that he loved me too much to do anything to hurt me.

This was about a year into the relationship and you would think after all the arguments (and there were A LOT), mental and emotional strain this relationship had caused me I would be all for walking away. Nope! I stuck around! I stuck around even after he stole more money from me, wrecked two of my cars, and inflicted some serious emotional and mental abuse. Sheesh! I tolerated it all and lost all peace of mind just to be able to say *I belonged*. Let me tell you this, there's nothing or no one that's worth losing your peace of mind over. After two and a half tumultuous years, he was sentenced to six months in jail and I took that opportunity to leave. God had orchestrated situations before that should have pushed me out the door, but I made the decision to stay. The decision to leave this time was fairly easy, but staying away from him is what required discipline. So, there I was, single and not belonging AGAIN! This time around was different though. Yes, I was single, but I knew I belonged and I knew whom I belonged to – the Almighty God.

There's nothing wrong with wanting to belong. It's a part of our human nature, but we have to practice discernment in who we allow to take up space in our lives. The crazy thing about this journey of life is if we're not careful, we'll become entrapped in a hurtful relationship – a relationship that we once entered to fill a void or to replace something we've lost. Sometimes we forget that we already belong to the greatest family ever, God's family! Everyone wants to belong, whether it's in a family, with colleagues, or a group of peers, but when you know you belong to God, your relationship with him supersedes all others.

Encouraged to Empower

On your journey to belonging again, you may have to:

1. **Forgive yourself.** Learn to forgive yourself of past

   mistakes and mishaps and accept God's grace and

   mercy over your life.

   List things you need to forgive yourself of to

   surrender in prayer.

   _____

   _____

   _____

2. **Find a welcoming church home.** Remember the

   feeling of wanting to belong, that's where the body of

   Christ becomes essential. Find a church home that

   speaks to your spirit and lends to your spiritual growth

   and development.

   If not connected to a church, where might you go

   physically? What church can you connect with

   online to further feed your spirit?

_____

_____

_____

3. **Keep God at your center.** The more you dive into

His word and the more you understand His

unconditional love, the more you will be able to feed

your appetite to belong.

How often do you currently spend in devotion

time? What can you do differently for more in-

depth studying?

_____

_____

_____

_____

You will find your spiritual group/community to be very

beneficial. It may require a bit of transparency and

vulnerability, but that doesn't necessarily mean you have to

blast all of your business and feelings either. However, you

will experience a weight release by doing so, as they can

also walk and pray with you on your journey.

Pray with Me

Heavenly Father, Thank You for reminding me of who I belong to. Your protection is always present and your love is immeasurable. I declare a feeling of belonging by way of Your kingdom.

The lost coin of belonging has now been found.
Let us rejoice in the name of Jesus. Amen.

Solid in You

"Therefore if any man be in Christ, he is a new creature: old things are passed away; behold, all things are become new."
~2 Corinthians 5:17, KJV~

It was the year 2013, and I had no clue who I was as a human being or as a child of God. My identity...ha! Yeah, there was no identity. I felt like a sponge, soaking up other's identities and trying to create some unique identity that I could call my own. Outside of my role as teacher, sister, and friend, my identity at the core was not solidified. I set out to have my identity redeveloped through friendships, which were more so acquaintances. If you've ever struggled with who you are, you are not alone. Many of us, throughout our lives, have lost a sense of who we are at the core. While this often leads to a never-ending cycle of bad decision-making, there is a way out – and it begins with being Solid in You – the You God created you to be.

I met people outside of work, and began putting them in my "friendship" pool. In developing these so-called friendships, I thought I could rediscover myself, attain an identity. Instead of seeking God and falling in love with myself, I went back out there in this crazy world searching for friendships to rediscover something that God had created. You would think by now I would have learned my lesson because doing it this way had definitely not been beneficial in the past. You know the saying, "The definition of insanity is continuing to do the same thing but expecting different results." I guess I was going through a phase of insanity.

I thought I knew all there was to know about friendships. I mean, we've been making friends since kindergarten, right? There's a big difference in healthy friendships and people that are just taking up space in your life. The people I considered friends were more like acquaintances. I was not entering into healthy situations. I was making acquaintances and just slapping the friendship title on there so that it looked more appeasing. Not really sure who I thought I was fooling or who I was trying to impress. I became friends, at least that's what I called it at the time, with a couple of people and we would text back and forth and occasionally go out to eat. That's it. That was the "friendship".

There was no substance in those situations and what I've learned over time is there has to be some kind of substance in any relationship. We shared some commonalities like sports, going out to eat, and certain television shows, but that was all. And yes, that's what I was basing my friendship on. There was no talk about church or our spiritual journey. There was no talk about long-term goals. Again, no substance. It was like sitting down to eat dinner but there's only cakes and pies on the table. Where's the chicken and potatoes? (lol... Sorry, I love food)

But seriously, there was nothing that would stick to your bones (as the old people say) and leave you feeling full. That's what those situations were, all dessert. We just existed in each other's presence. We weren't challenging each other to be better versions of ourselves. We were literally just taking up space in each other's lives. This became obvious when I moved from St. Louis to Houston and those connections dwindled away. The biggest revelation through all of this is that I was ultimately trying to figure out who I was through these "friendships". There were several instances, but one situation stands out the most during this time.

I went out to dinner with a "friend" and the conversation started off well talking about sports, but then the conversation turned dull. I remember sitting there thinking what in the world am I doing here. I tried to steer the conversation towards God, life goals, or our careers and nothing happened. There was no feedback or additional dialogue. It was weird! I literally sat there like, "Ummm, are you going to respond?" That's when I knew I had fallen into a rut of nothingness.

I learned that I would never be able to find my identity through other people because I was not created by people. I needed to devote time to myself. We cannot look to other people to determine our identity; we have to look to our Creator, the one who created us for a purpose. Instead of chatting with God on how to get my identity back and what I should do next, I planned out my next steps by myself. (A little side note: don't ever try to plan your next steps without talking to God first). Proverbs 19:21 states, "Many are the plans in a person's heart, but it is the Lord's purpose that prevails." When we try to plan our next steps without God, we're literally wasting time and energy.

After some deep conversations with God, I realized I just needed to step back. This wasn't a time to be on the prowl for friendships because those friendships weren't going to address the real problem, which was me needing to learn me all over again and figure out who I was. This was the time to be focused on self. Now, that doesn't mean I just dropped all acquaintances when this was revealed. Yeah, I'm a little more hard-headed than that.

I was still looking for someone or a group of people to fill voids. If you find yourself in this place, please, for the love of God forgive yourself. You are not perfect – none of us are. If we were, we wouldn't need God. Now, I'm not saying friendships aren't a good thing or unnecessary – just the contrary. The right friendships, for the right reasons, are very much necessary and needed. Friendships are to enhance

26

and strengthen who you are, but they should not define you. The only person that loves you better or more than you is God. So with that being said, fall in love with yourself honey! Enjoy being in the company of yourself and embracing the love of God. Many times in life we look to people to fill voids and we end up in meaningless friendships and/or relationships. As I mentioned before, there is absolutely no one that can love you better than yourself or God. Let's get back to loving ourselves

Encouraged to Empower

I cannot stress enough how important it is to fall in love with yourself. In fact that's my first word of encouragement, so let's start there.

1. **Fall in love with yourself.** Love who you are as a person. All of your quirks, silly ways, whatever it is that makes you unique, Love It! We are all different. We were created to be unique. Sometimes we may go through situations where we lose sight of this, but it is in these moments where we have to reassess. There is so much about you to love. Jesus died on the cross because of his love for you.

   What are some things about you that you should love that you haven't always loved?

   _____

   _____

   _____

2. **Establish some healthy hobbies.** Discover what makes your spirit happy. If you're not sure because

you've grown accustomed to everyone else's hobbies, that's okay. Venture out and explore. There's so much out there to see. Once you discover healthy hobbies, commit to doing at least one per week. I know you may say, "I don't have time for that", but if you don't pause and make time to get reacquainted with yourself you will forever be basing your identity on those around you.

How have you misidentified yourself based on someone else's opinion?

_____

_____

_____

_____

3. **Get to know you again.** When you go through a phase of adopting other people's persona, you lose your God-given identity. Take time to rediscover your passion for things you used to do or you may become introduced to activities you didn't even realized you'd enjoy.

What are some things you're passionate about that you've laid aside, but would love to enjoy again?

_____

_____

_____

These are just a few steps to how you begin the journey of re-identifying yourself. Your identity is not based on anyone else's hobbies, their likes or dislikes; it's based on you! I became comfortable with going to nice restaurants, to the movies, art museums, and to parks by myself. I figured out what I liked, what made my spirit happy. People may question your why, but you don't owe anyone an explanation about the decisions you are making to better yourself. It's not weird or strange; it's you falling back in love with yourself.

Pray with Me

Heavenly Father, Thank You for loving me before I knew how to love myself. You died for us and welcomed us into Your family as sinners. There is truly no greater love. Being a member of the family of the Host High could bring us a feeling of fullness, if we accept all that is being offered to us. Father God, help us to accept the invitation to be a member of the one and only Royal Family. Thank You for your constant reminder of how much we are loved and adored by You.

> The lost coin of identity has now been found.
> Let us rejoice in the name of Jesus. Amen.

~About Karena~

Karena Washington currently resides in Houston, TX as a 4th grade teacher. She is certified in EC-6, Special Education, and ESL. She received her Masters in Teaching from Fontbonne University and has been teaching for seven years. She has worked with kids ages 5-18 in various settings, including a developmental center, a juvenile center, and in the educational setting since 2001.

Karena has a passion for working with kids and helping them become the best version of themselves. Having been awarded with Teacher of the Year during the 2016-17 school year at Parkway Central Middle School in Missouri, she is grateful for the opportunities afforded to impact the lives of many young people.

In 2019, she began offering tutoring services through her business, Unabridged. Her mission is to help kids in grades K-6 improve and strengthen their reading skills.

For more info, please visit www.unabridgedsolutions.com.

Not Your Typical Foodie

You formed my innermost being, shaping my delicate inside and my intricate outside, and wove them all together in my mother's womb. I thank you, God, for making me so mysteriously complex! Everything you do is marvelously breathtaking. It simply amazes me to think about it! How thoroughly you know me, Lord!
~Psalms 139:13-14 (TPT)~

Have you ever had a brownie fresh out of the oven? Did you enjoy the taste of the warm gooey chocolate treat in your mouth? Did you love how it made you feel? Were you so wrapped up in that brownie that you hated the feeling of emptiness after it was gone so quickly? You decide, 'Well, there's no harm in having another one' because the first brownie was so good and gone so quick. Then the same thing happens again. So you have a third, a fourth, then a fifth. Next thing you know the whole freaking pan is gone and you feel like your stomach is going to burst open in an explosion of guts and chocolate. This was a common thing for me with everything that I ate. One would think that simply deciding to not eat a dozen of brownies in one sitting would be easy. But, I was 'Not Your Typical Foodie'!

Food was my first love and my first heartbreak. As a child, I relied on food to help me deal with everything. Whenever I was sad (which was often), I ate. Whenever I was angry, I ate. Even in the moments in which I was happy (which was rare), I ate. I even ate through my constant nervousness. I was never one to have a lot of friends. Social interaction had always been so hard for me. I could never understand how people worked, or how I was supposed to operate among them. So food became my friend in order to cope with the loneliness. I am what one would call an emotional eater. Any emotion that I could not or chose not to understand, I used food to cope with it instead. There are so many memories I have of myself as a child crying and eating at the same time. I would literally stuff my mouth through tears and weeping, often time choking from the combination of the food and sniffling.

I had always felt insignificant or unimportant to the world around me. It was as if everything around me was moving forward in a fast pace and I couldn't keep up. I felt like everything was out of my control and no one cared if I was being left behind - no one cared about me at all. But *food* made me feel special. The feeling I got from eating on my favorite food was the same feeling I so desperately wanted to feel from someone else. Any other time, I felt worthless. I just wanted to feel like I mattered, and in those moments when I was alone with my food, I did matter.

Of course, this harmful habit only created a toxic cycle for me that worsened each time it renewed itself. The pounds would just pile on because of my excessive eating, I'd get triggered into an emotional spiral as a result of my weight, and then I'd turn around and binge on more food to cope with the emotional spiral. Even as I got heavier and heavier, my meals would get bigger and more harmful. The emotions I refused to deal with properly only became wilder and harder to handle.

My triggers also became increasingly more sensitive. Most of my binging triggers surfaced in the form of bullying. When I was in school, other kids made me the receiver of their insults and the butt of their repetitive fat and colorist jokes. I remember this one particular kid ALWAYS had something to say about me. It didn't matter the time or place (classroom, cafeteria, playground, a field trip). This kid always had a fat joke locked, loaded and ready to aim at me. The other kids were mean, but this particular kid was relentless.

Unfortunately, the fat comments didn't stop with the kids at school. Some of my family members were the source of my torment. My childhood was plagued with the complicated feelings surrounding my father and his side of the family. I had two younger brothers who lived with my father (one less than a year younger than me and the other about five years younger than me). The brother that was closer to my age would always call me fat and the youngest one would just follow his lead. We were kids and my brothers were just operating from their own hurt, but that didn't make the insults sting any less for me.

Needless to say, the feelings of worthlessness were always heightened during my weekend visits with my father. For a long time, I genuinely hated being around my family. Such a strong emotion for an elementary school age child to feel, but it was true. I absolutely dreaded the moments leading up to my father knocking on the door to pick me up. I remember I would sit and nervously eat on a sugar filled Little Debbie snack or two while I waited for him. By the time I returned home on Sunday night, I would be feeling so low, all I wanted to do was gorge myself on whatever was in the kitchen.

As you can imagine, I was an incredibly sad child. I think most people could tell I was sad in general, but I do not think anyone knew the depth of how sad I actually was. At the age of eleven, I had the first concrete thought of 'I want to die'. I actually feared death a little less and viewed it more as an escape – just at the age of eleven.

The horrendous habit of making food my refuge was something that stayed with me throughout the rest of my childhood, adolescence, and into my adulthood. By June of 2019, my weight had peaked at 237 pounds, which I did not carry well on my 5'3 frame. I was 23 and in the worst place in my life. By this time I had landed myself into a very toxic relationship and food alone was no longer enough to help me cope. I had added alcohol now to my gluttonous ritual.

I went from drinking on some weekends, to drinking every weekend, to drinking almost every day. There were days when I would take a couple of shots before class just to get through the day. Being a college student and relying heavily on alcohol to function normally is not an ideal situation.

I had reached a point in my life where food and alcohol were steadily becoming less helpful with my issues. My sadness became harder for me to control. My emotions got so wild that I would have outbursts at times in which I absolutely needed to keep control. One semester, I had an anxiety attack in the middle of my final exam. I remember barely holding myself together long enough until I made it out the building to hide and hyperventilate by a dumpster. My suicidal thoughts had evolved as well. I went from simply thinking I want to die' to contemplating all of the ideal ways in which I wanted to die and how I would want my body to be handled. I wanted a straight cremation. My self worth was so low that I didn't even think that I was worth the hassle of a funeral. At this point, if I were to compile all of the 'last letters' I had written throughout the years, the stack would be enough to create an anthology, with three volumes for childhood, adolescent, and adulthood. I still carry the scars from some of my attempts.

From the start, I knew I had mental issues that I'd neglected for years. I knew that these same issues played a big role in my relationship with food. I was blessed to be attending a university that offered free counseling services to students. For the first time, I got names assigned to my vortex of emotions: high functioning depression and anxiety. I had always used food to ease the emptiness I felt. Learning that I had depression helped so much because I was able to logically conclude that food will never fill that void. Mental illness can only be helped through therapy, medication, and prayer. Food was never going to help me hate myself less.

What I've learned is that a lack of self-awareness and a heavy dose of denial can lead a person to pick up some seriously unhealthy vices. The focus that I learned to put on my mental health led to me taking my physical health seriously.

Encouraged to Empower

Life can become too much sometimes, so much so that we often lose our grip, which leads into a downward spiral. While there's so much more you can do, these three things helped me regain control:

1. **Journal Your Prayers.** It is important to contemplate and plan with God. Journaling prayers can help with the beginning stage of overcoming whatever you are struggling with. Whatever revelations you have reached with God will be on paper making it easy to reference back to when you need it. *God has a one track mind as far as we are concerned. He wants us to live like the overcomers that we are. (Corinthians 5:6-9, TPT).*

   What are reasons you wouldn't journal? What can you do in place of journaling to record your prayers?

   _____

   _____

   _____

2. **Ignore the outside.** Your journey is between you and God. Do not let anyone take you from your path of finding your own lost coin. You may very well be surprised of the people in your life who will be threatened by your journey and your growth. You have to ignore it nonetheless.

   Who (or what) have you found to be a distraction to your growth journey? What can you do to minimize these distractions?

   _____

   _____

   _____

   _____

3. **Remind Yourself To Keep Going.** Do everything you can to remind yourself of your end goal. Keep talking to God. Write yourself sticky notes of encouragement and put them everywhere you can. Even talk to yourself in the mirror if need be. Remind yourself that you are capable of being your best you. You are worthy of reaching the end of your journey.

   What can you write on sticky notes or your mirror for encouragement? (instead of writing here, actually write on sticky notes, note cards, or mirror)

Self-awareness and clarity are so important. When we're lacking in these areas, we find ourselves only attacking symptoms as opposed to the root issues.

Pray with Me

Father God, Thank You for the gift of being self-aware through clarity and change in perspective. You allow challenges so that I can grow, but you never give me more than what I can handle. When life seems to be spinning out of control, I am able to step back, breath, and evaluate. Father God, you have given me the tools to grow as an individual.

The lost coin of self-awareness has now been found.
Let us rejoice in the name of Jesus. Amen.

Loving God So I Can Love Myself

*"There is no greater love than the love that holds on where
there seems nothing left to hold on to."*
~1 Corinthians 13:8, NIV~

I made a decision a few years back that I regret *severely*. I lost my virginity at the age of 20 to some guy so that I would feel like a woman. What I realize now is that sex isn't what makes a woman. One's character, growth, and faith are traits that really define a woman. If I knew then what I knew now, I would've saved myself a lot of heartbreak and mental breakdowns.

It was 2016 and I was 20 years old. I had somehow convinced myself that I was ready to have sex because of my age. I thought I was too old to still be a virgin. 'Twenty is old enough,' I had told myself. However, I had neglected to consider that maybe I wasn't mentally or emotionally ready to endure the consequences that would follow.

Unsurprisingly, when I picked some boy at my university to lose my virginity to, I felt no positive change afterwards. In fact, I felt worse. I didn't feel the big entrance into womanhood that I thought I would. Honestly, I felt more like a child than ever. My already low self-esteem plummeted, as I felt I didn't have much to offer and had now stupidly tossed away what little value I had.

From that moment on I operated out of desperation. I was desperate to replace my loss of purity with validation and love from someone else. I needed someone to tell me that I was still worthy of love. Unfortunately, this led me down the wrong path for a while. I ended up in several unhealthy relationships and flings. I let people who didn't even deserve to touch me use my body for their own short-lived amusement. My search for love and validation was really a path of self-destruction. It all came to a head with the end of a toxic relationship involving a narcissist.

I endured that relationship because I had convinced myself that was the closest thing to love I'd ever experience. During this relationship I leaned on unhealthy vices like overeating and alcohol to cope with life. My depression and anxiety eclipsed all other emotions and thoughts I had. I hadn't known genuine happiness in such a long time. I'm sad to say that my wake-up call only came when I walked in on my then partner in bed with another woman.

Even though I was tired, I was in one toxic relationship after another. It didn't matter if they were romantic, platonic, or otherwise.

The moment I walked in on that horrible scene was the moment I realized that it had to stop. These situations I kept putting myself in for the sake of feeling loved needed to stop. That incident marked the end of that relationship and the end of dating for me. I immediately decided to become celibate the moment I ended that last relationship. The desperation for external validation ran so deep for me that the beginning of my journey to heal and regain what was lost was so grueling and difficult.

There was one emotional breakthrough after another. I juggled between crying and rage and hopelessness so much, I didn't know if I was going to make it to the other side of my hurt. I wanted badly to unsex myself in every sense of the word and somehow magically get my purity back. Even still, I came out on the other side of my healing journey as a new woman with new values. My value is what I make it, regardless of the status of my virginity. Through my prayers and conversations with God I finally understood that God loves me unconditionally. That love was worth more than anything that I could get from a man.

For anyone reading my story, I hope you gain an understanding of what it means to love yourself. I do not want anyone to think that I am trying to shove my own way of life down their throats, or that the only way to live a life fulfilled is to be celibate. I am sharing my diamonds because I want for the next young black girl who is wrestling with insecurities to learn from my mistakes. No one should ever look to another earthly human being for any sense of validation or importance. I know we hear that often, but one should always look within as well as to God for unconditional love. This perspective will save many of our girls from so much unnecessary pain and drama.

Encouraged to Empower

Self-worth is so important. Having a sense of self-worth is what allows you to embrace all of the best things about yourself and accept all of the not so great things about yourself. Consider these things as you embrace who you are:

1. **Talk to God.** Before you do anything talk to God first. Do it by prayer, conversation, or journaling if you have to. Talk to God in times of need, times of hardships, and times of joy. Talking and planning with God is essential to starting the journey to finding your self-worth.

   What ways have you found most comfortable to communicate with God? How can you stretch yourself beyond these methods?

   _____

   _____

   _____

   _____

2. **Don't Compromise.** Love yourself enough to no longer compromise what you value the most. Know that you can do anything you put your mind to according to God's will.

What values have you compromised? What parameters/boundaries can you put in place to avoid further compromises?

_____

_____

_____

_____

_____

3. **Look in the Mirror.** The mirror is the best place to go to so you can look that person straight in the eyes and let her know that you are fearfully and wonderfully made. You must speak the Word of God over your life as that is the foundation for who you are: Chosen, Loved, Accepted, and more!

When you look in the mirror what do you see? Is it how God sees you? If not, what can you do to change your perspective?

_____

_____

_____

While some of these may seem challenging at first, especially looking in the mirror, the more you make these a part of your daily routine, the easier you'll find it to love yourself. You'll also become more mindful of how deep and unconditional God's love is for you.

Pray with Me

Father God, Thank You for the gift of life. Thank you for always reminding me of how precious life can be. Thank you for renewed strength and self-worth. Thank you for taking me out of harmful environments and placing me in the safe haven that is Your love and light. I am Your Daughter!

The lost coin of self-worth has now been found.
Let us rejoice in the name of Jesus. Amen.

~About Tatiana~

Tatiana Glass is a first-time author. She is passionate about all things involving creative writing, including novels and screenplays. She is one of the creators behind Black Writers Anonymous, an organization dedicated to providing a safe space and platform for black writers to create and develop their writing.

Tatiana can be contacted at tzglass19@gmail.com.

Turn on the Light

Before I formed thee in the belly I knew thee; and before thou camest forth out of the womb I sanctified thee, and I ordained thee a prophet unto the nations.
~Jeremiah 1:5, KJV~

The lights are off. It's pitch-black. I can't find a way out of here. It seems like the doors are closed. I am empty shouting on the inside, and no one can hear me. I am so dirty and disgusting, a bath couldn't clean me up. "Why did you have to do me like that? I was innocent until you touched me." Please help me find a light switch... Someone please turn on the light...

My dreams were always to be a gymnast. At the age of eight, I loved doing back flips, hand stands and splits, imagining myself being in the Olympics. I mean I could do the Chinese splits and flip off the trunk of a car. I could do round offs and backbends. I knew if I kept practicing I could be on television. My two oldest brothers would let me flip from their hands. I loved gymnastics until one day everything changed.

My mom's favorite cousin came over one day. He was in his late 20's. This was the day my life became dark. She left him with us while she went to the store. He told me to come into the room where it was just me and him. He began to take my panties off and started to put his mouth on my private area. He used Vaseline and started to put his penis in me. I remember it was big and it hurt. My private area was so swollen I had to sit at the dinner table with my legs open straddling the corner of the chair. I could barely walk I was in so much pain, but he told me not to tell or he would hurt me and my family.

This attack on my innocence began at the age of eight and continued until I was twelve years old. At the age of twelve I told my sister that our cousin molested me. She told my mom, and I was beat in my back. She was so angry with me because I didn't tell her, but I didn't feel I had a voice. I was so afraid that he would hurt me or them. She confronted him and he admitted to molesting me, but claimed he was drunk. I never went and got a check-up. I was so afraid I wouldn't be able to have babies, or that I might have contracted a sexual transmitted disease. I didn't know how to express myself and thus began the anger issues. Fighting became my outlet, my release.

I had to complete the seventh grade three times due to being expelled so many times for fighting. I was the bully to the bullies. I wasn't afraid of anyone. But deep down I felt dirty, impure, and unclean, as I was no longer a virgin; I wouldn't be able to call anyone my first. Imagine living with your eyes open, yet you feel so blind. That was me. My self-worth was gone, and I didn't trust anyone.

I started drinking straight gin and you know what they say, "Gin make you sin". It was not enough for me. I was consuming so much alcohol at an early age, my mom said to me one day, "I heard you been drinking. Can you please add some water to it?" She knew I was going to do what I wanted to do, so she suggested I add water to the liquor so it wouldn't be too hard on my body.

I started feeling so confused, not knowing if I liked girls or boys. I started having sex at 14 years old and got pregnant at 15. My son was born two months before my

16th birthday. His dad and I eventually broke up two years later. I started being promiscuous and commitment was not in my vocabulary. I did not care if a man was in a relationship or not, I wanted what I wanted. I did not have many partners, but it was enough to count on one hand.

Being molested was extremely hard to overcome. I was so lost with feelings of unworthiness. Drinking and sex became my coping mechanisms, but I eventually regained my self-worth and strength to move forward. I refused to stay in the dark, and decided to turn on the light. I realized my worth was more than the molestation experienced. I began to acknowledge my bad, destructive behaviors and forgave myself.

I forgave myself for thinking I was not good enough, for believing I would be nothing. I started loving *me* again by establishing standards and setting boundaries. I wanted to prepare myself to be somebody's wife. So, I stopped accepting bad behavior and disrespect from other people. I learned to say no and chose to live again.

Encouraged to Empower

What I want you to know is just because bad things happened to you, it doesn't mean you have to continue living in darkness. There is always a light on the inside of you, but you will have to be the one to turn it back on.

1. **Accept the Lord Jesus Christ as your Savior.** This is the beginning of a new life. Confess out of your mouth and believe he died on the cross for your sin. Your heart must be willing and ready to receive him. Jesus can treat you better than anybody. John 3:16 shares, *For God so loved the world, that he gave his only begotten Son, that whosoever believeth in him should not perish, but have everlasting life.*

   Have you accepted Jesus Christ as your Savior? If not, please feel free to reach out to one of us here to help you begin your journey.

2. **Don't Settle.** Love yourself enough to not settle for disrespect. Have confidence in yourself to know that you can do anything you put your mind to.

What have you been settling for? Why have you settled? What needs to happen for you to no longer settle?

_____

_____

_____

_____

_____

3. **Encourage Yourself.** The mirror is the best place to go to so you can look that person straight in the eyes and let her or him know that you are fearfully and wonderfully made. You must speak the word of God over your life as it gives you strength. Be reminded of Philippians 4:13 which says, *I can do all things through Christ which strengtheneth me.*

Find a scripture/passage that you can refer back to for encouragement when feeling discouraged, down, or frustrated. Write it here.

_____

_____

_____

As you take these steps to regain your self-worth, you will also find that what you've endured can serve as a platform to help someone else overcome feelings of unworthiness.

Pray with Me

Father God, thank you for reminding me that I have the power to turn my lights back on. Thank you for reminding me who I am in you, and that I belong to you. Thank you for renewed strength and self-worth. Thank you for not only bringing me out of abusive situations, but also restoring that which the enemy tried to take. I am Your Daughter!

The lost coin of self-worth has now been found.
Let us rejoice in the name of Jesus. Amen.

Exposing Greatness

I will praise thee; for I am fearfully and wonderfully made: marvelous are thy works; and that my soul knoweth right well.
~Psalm 139:14, KJV~

"We delight in the beauty of the butterfly, but rarely admit the changes it has gone through to achieve that beauty." (Maya Angelou) Life is like a metamorphosis, where you don't know the finish product until it goes through the changes of life. The beginning of life is fun, curious, and full of learning until adversity comes and everything around you becomes darkened and different. Your vision becomes blurry and blinded leaving you searching for your identity in people, places, and things. As God would have it however, sometimes these are the things necessary to expose your greatness.

What a gift to the world, pure joy and laughter? I remember loving to love and gathering everyone around. I enjoyed making others happy even at my own expense. However, I was secretly exhausted from saying *yes* to everybody's command. Even if I didn't like it, if they were happy that was all that mattered. I just loved to serve and help, but some of the people I did for did not appreciate it.

I felt used at times and taken advantage of. They knew if they called on me I would do whatever was asked. I believe in my early 20's I was considered 'green' because people would call me for bill money and I'd graciously give it. They'd ask to borrow money from me, and I'd graciously give, but would never get it back. I was invited to many churches for speaking engagements, as they knew I would bring the people. This too was just another way people preyed on me. I felt like I was being hustled, but I really wanted people to get saved. I had so many different leaders with some good and not so good experiences. Overall, however, they taught me what to do and what not to do when it came to serving and leading people.

I got tired of church. Some leaders were intimidated by my anointing and didn't want me doing anything in the church. I just wanted them to see me. I went to church on time, I was at every Bible Study, Sunday School, and every event. I was so excited about God and felt like I was a natural born leader. Yet, I struggled with the need for validation to affirm my purpose and my spiritual growth walk.

I was rejected by a pastor because he did not trust his leaders. It was very seldom that he would let other ministers preach. He would always fuss in the pulpit, and I remember thinking, 'Can this man at least give me a scripture so I can have something to eat?' I don't know why people fussed in the pulpit, just give us the word.

I found myself frustrated with Church because of cliques talking about people and leaders sleeping with members of their congregation. Eventually, I decided to start church at my home. I did it one time and five people were in attendance. That was the beginning of my ministry and I began to go live on Facebook, and it was just a blessing. I also started having Bible Study at the library. People began coming out and it was a success. I never knew what was going to be next.

While teaching, a man that knew the Word began to help teach at the library with me. It was so exciting. The word of God was going forth and it was growing with a lot of people from my Facebook, people that personally knew me, or people I had previously ministered to.

One day my sister said to me, "You know there's a church for rent and I think you and that guy you're doing Bible Study with would do good together." A seed was planted. I'd never thought about opening a church. My confidence was not where it needed to be, so I thought I needed a male because a lot of people didn't believe in women pastors. I also knew the landlord over the church wouldn't consider just me. I was afraid to talk to the landlord myself, so I asked the man helping me with the Bible Study to go with me. The minute this man put his feet over the threshold of the church, it became evident he had his own vision. I had my own as well, and it was not church as usual in the traditional sense.

Because my confidence was low, I chose a partner that was deceitful, a liar and a manipulator. I trusted this person with the finances, and he created a board that wanted to have me removed. How funny since I was the one paying the church bills. If he didn't like something, he would sabotage it and try to force people to agree with him. The final straw of frustration happened when he called a meeting and said he had me on recording. He said he couldn't talk to me because I wouldn't listen. I was so hurt because I didn't know he was secretly recording our conversations. I had nothing to hide because it was only from a business level, but I was so offended that someone in ministry, someone I'd joined with to serve God's people, was not trustworthy.

I had to find a way to get out or to separate from this person. I did a demerging agreement with him where he would have service on one day, and I'd have service another day. It was a challenging experience thinking I needed a partner to get a building, when all along I didn't need him as expected. I had to stay in that church for a whole year with him, and it was one thing after another. One day he called the police on one of the members and he lied about that. He would look at the video from my days in service and come to harass us. It was a horrible experience, but my confidence in self was just not there.

When you are so giving, not to mention a people-pleaser, many will take advantage of you. Eventually, it leaves you frustrated, angry, and often times becomes the end of friendships. When you want to be validated by people, you find yourself competing and comparing yourself to others, which heightens your levels of self-doubt. In addition, low self-confidence affects good decision-making that will cost you your peace. But to God be the glory as He has a way of turning things around for his glory. In spite of the misuse, betrayal, and ugliness of situations, God will always see to it that your greatness is exposed.

Encouraged to Empower

It's stated in Genesis that God was the creator of all things and all things he made was good. That includes You. While others may not see or acknowledge your greatness, know that God does. Hopefully, these points will help expose your own levels of greatness.

1. **Be a pleaser of God.** One thing I can share for certain is you'll never go wrong pleasing God for he is your number one fan and supporter. Deuteronomy 31:6 reminds us that he never leaves or forsakes us. Not only that, he truly has your best interest at heart Every Single Day! There is great truth in the Matthew 6:33 passage that tells us to seek first his kingdom and righteousness and he will give us all we need. Please God first; taste and see that the Lord is good (Psalm 34:8) and rest assured he will never betray your kindness, time, or generosity.

What are ways you can please God?

_____

_____

_____

2. **Self-Love and acceptance.** Loving and accepting yourself begins with you changing the lens of how you see yourself. Consider that you're a daughter of the Most High and that carries great weight. He was specific in his intricate design of you and he makes no mistakes.

   Write out words (and even back-up scripture) that describe how God sees you to say to yourself when needed.

   _____

   _____

   _____

3. **Self-Validation.** Your key to self-validation begins with your own beliefs, thoughts, and words. At the end of each day, take a moment to consider what rubbed you the wrong way and how you could've perceived it

differently. Tackling the why behind your feelings each day helps to quench the need for others to validate you.

What are some faulty beliefs you've held on to that led to the need of validation from others? How can you rewrite those beliefs?

_____

_____

_____

_____

_____

So much more awaits you, and God has already equipped you to move forward in purpose. While you're not meant to do everything alone, know that people are simply a complement to your gifts, not the ultimate resource, which is God.

Pray with Me

Father God, thank you for reminding me of my greatness as according to your Word. You are an awesome God who has never let me down nor taken me for granted. Thank you for seeing who I am at the core. Thank you for choosing me, for validating me, for wanting me, and keeping me. You are my encourager, my comforter, my friend, and confidant.

The lost coin of acceptance has now been found.
Let us rejoice in the name of Jesus. Amen.

~About Ronnetta~

Apostle Ronnetta Rockamore is no stranger to the ministry. Although she was ordained in December 2011, she didn't accept the role until January 2019. She has been ministering for over 23 years with a very energetic, pioneer, and warrior type spirit. Since her ministry is not created for walls, she is able to minister to those in the prisons, nursing homes, streets, door to door, and more.

She loves spending time with her family, which includes her husband, Tythann Rockamore, and their three children. She is currently the Senior Pastor at SoulFed Life Ministries, Inc. located in North Little Rock, Arkansas. She graduated with an Arts and Science Degree and recently completed her certification as a Life Coach.

Apostle Ronnetta can be contacted at

ronnettajones1@gmail.com.

The Awakening

"Am I now trying to win the approval of human beings, or of God? Or am I trying to please people? If I were still trying to please people, I would not be a servant of Christ".
~ Galatians 1:10, NIV ~

Have you ever lost anything? Your keys, cell phone, your job? When losing these things, you begin to search in many different places such as your car, bathroom, closet, or countertop. You may explore the internet, seek the unemployment office, or inquire from friends of any openings. Most of us have lost something, but have you ever lost your confidence, your joy, yourself? Well, I lost myself to the point that dysfunction became part of my everyday life. *Yes man* was my name, and people pleasing was my game. I lost my identity saying *yes* to please people, while not realizing I was saying *no* to me. In the moment of my awakening, I knew that something had to change.

Understanding my being a people-pleaser in retrospect began at age twelve with a desire for approval. I was hungry for approval – something I had lacked even before the age of twelve. As an adult, I found myself going out of my way and sacrificing my own family needs to accommodate other people. I failed to exercise the boundary of saying NO because I feared the backlash. The guilt of disappointing others seemed too heavy to carry, but I failed to acknowledge how God tells us to cast our anxiety on him because he loves us (1 Peter 5:7, NIV).

In the Summer of 2018, I found myself lost, depressed, angry, and trying to figure out where I belonged. The previous year I had left my church of 17 years, which was a large part of my identity. I sought emotional support from a women's empowerment group. I wanted to explore where my pain was coming from. I was so excited and relieved after speaking with a representative of the group about what I was feeling. She seemed to know exactly what I was going through, and without hesitation, we scheduled a phone consultation for that Saturday at 12:00 p.m. I soon realized I'd scheduled the call the same day as my daughter's basketball game, but I could not disappoint the representative. The day came for our meeting, and feeling empowered, I awaited the call. I sent my daughter off to her game with her father. Unfortunately, 12:00 p.m. came and went. No call, no text, just disappointment.

A few weeks later, even after my disappointment, I found myself saying *yes* again. I was asked by the same representative – who had not apologized for disrespecting my time previously – to assist with her group. In my dysfunction of wanting to please, she spoke to my need for approval and I gladly answered the call. All over again, I was doing something that gave momentary comfort because I felt needed. That made me feel good about myself. Again, I allowed that to taint my relationship with the people I loved. I failed to attend another one of my daughter's basketball games due to my desire to serve someone else – not myself, or my family, but someone else. To add insult to injury, she failed to call yet again, and I came to realize that I was being treated less than my value. Everything that was anything connected to me, I felt was being disrespected and overlooked, therefore devalued. This was my wake-up call. I sought the Lord and asked Him, "What is wrong with me?"

The answer did not come immediately, but it came on time at this very moment as I was preparing my thoughts to write this story.

He answered me by revealing that I was co-dependent, a term I knew very little about. I realized, however, I was living a life with poor boundaries, people-pleasing tendencies, and low-self-esteem. What was wrong with me is I was co-dependent. I rejoiced and thanked God for the revelation, for enlightening me and giving my long-held feelings a name with release. I was now able to express my pent-up thoughts and feelings, and it became easier to talk to my husband about what was going on with me. I felt the shift in my body as my shoulders began to relax from the weight of the stress I had carried. I asked God to forgive me for neglecting the family that He gave me due to my co-dependency and need to please others. I also asked God to forgive me for allowing myself to be devalued.

After seeking God's wisdom and forgiveness, I committed my deliverance from people-pleasing and the patterns of co-dependency to the Lord. Proverbs 16:3 tells us to, "Commit to the Lord whatever you do, and he will establish your plans." Depending on God's power and strength was essential to my recovery. I was able to find and reaffirm my identity in God. I, Sharifa Stirgus, am a lavishly loved child of God (1 John 3:1, NIV). I am a servant of Christ who is to serve to glorify God and not man. Also, it is by the daily renewal of my mind through God's Word and practicing saying *no* to activities and people that pull me away from God, my family, and myself, that I have found that most valuable lost coin – my identity in Christ.

After repeated disappointments in my quest to gain and keep the love, sense of belonging, and approval I thought I needed, I was awakened. I was reminded that I had been seeking the wrong thing and was reaping what I had sown. God tells us to seek first His kingdom and His righteousness and all these things will be given to you as well (Matthew 6:33, NIV). God will not disappoint us. Because of my awakening and renewed identity in God, I am breaking the chains of co-dependency and people-pleasing in my daily life with faith in God and much prayer.

Encouraged to Empower

To my beloved sisters, I want to encourage you to not allow yourself or others take you away from your first gift, which is your family.

Here are steps I practice daily, and I pray they will help you on your journey of overcoming co-dependency and people-pleasing.

1. ***Seek God's approval and not men.*** God is our Rock that we can lean and depend on at any given time. Ask God before joining a women's group or any other activity to see if it will benefit you and/or your family in a healthy way. Proverbs 3:5-6 tells you to trust in the Lord completely, and do not rely on your own opinions. With all your heart rely on him to guide you, and he will lead you in every decision you make (TPT).

   How far would you go to please others?

   _____

   _____

2. ***Love yourself enough to respect the value of your own time knowing you're also saying yes to self.*** You can do this by treating yourself to a spa day, an evening of going shopping or just as simple as buying yourself your favorite meal where you can enjoy it all on your own.

   When is it your time?

   _____

   _____

3. ***Fact check your emotions and motives.*** When you feel uneasy or led to do something, ask yourself is it to receive approval from others. This will allow you to understand the true motives of your need to do.

   Should you do this for them or yourself?

   _____

   _____

Many people will come and go in your life for different seasons and reasons. They may be there to help you along the way, but their time does expire and is not always meant to be for a lifetime. This is something that we all must pay close attention to and not get caught up in the 'need-to-be-on-the-go' mentality because when you fall more than likely, your family or someone who is close to you will still be there to pick you up.

Pray with Me

Heavenly Father, Thank You for reminding me of who I am in you. Thank you for choosing me to be your friend. Thank you for loving me the way you do. Father I thank you for giving me the strength to set boundaries to say No and to overcome people-pleasing. Thank you for telling me in your word that I am valuable, more than enough for you and the apple of your eye. Thank you for allowing me to have a sense of belonging in you Jesus!

The lost coin of identity has now been found.
Let us rejoice in the name of Jesus. Amen.

Thine Will Be Done

*"This is the confidence we have in approaching God: that if
we ask anything according to his will, he hears us."*
~I John 5:14, NIV~

Life is like a riddle, a puzzling question full of uncertainty that
requires insight to uncover its true answer or meaning. How
many times have you questioned the meaning of life or
God's purpose for your life? Was the answer easy to find or
are you still searching for the answer? On the quest to follow
God's revelation and my dreams of becoming a nurse, I lost
my confidence due to invalidation from a series of setbacks
and failures, and was left with the puzzling question, "Whose
will is it anyway?" It was only through acceptance of God's
will over my own that I was able to regain my confidence.

Seven years ago, I was overcoming obstacles on my
mission to become a nurse. I had committed myself to an
intensive study schedule and tedious study tactics to
become the "perfect" student. In the Fall 2013 semester, I
successfully completed my prerequisite classes for nursing
school with a 4.0 GPA, earning Dean's List distinction each

semester, and being accepted into the Phi Theta Kappa Honor Society. All of this was achieved while working a full-time job, managing a household, and being a wife and mother of two girls. I was extremely proud of my achievements as a non-traditional student because I had last attended school 14 years prior. By the spring of 2014, I was preparing to take the Nursing Entrance Assessment Exam, which would determine if I were eligible to enter the nursing program. The time was challenging and stressful for me, but my hard work paid off. I passed my entrance exam and earned acceptance into the program. Surely, I thought, I must be doing the right thing.

During the first two months of nursing school in the fall of 2014, I began with a high level of self-assurance though I knew the journey was going to be very intense. My experience in the classroom was like the first day of a fitness boot camp. Only this left my mind sore all over from the weight of the tons of information the instructors loaded us with. I studied like a crazed woman. I found myself writing my notes three times, studying Monday through

Friday from 4:00 p.m.-11:00 p.m. and from 3:00 a.m.-5:00 a.m. Then I'd arrive to school by 7:00 a.m. with just enough time to study again before my 8:00 a.m. class started.

Staying up late at night and waking up to prayer time were my caffeine. I was pushing myself daily to make it through my class, but suddenly, I began to self-sabotage with thoughts of doubt even though I had previously been assured by the Lord. He showed me a vision of me attending nursing school before being admitted. Self-doubt was replacing my self-assurance, and financial stressors due to a job lay-off and needing to replace essential home appliances at a critical time intensified my anxiety.

I can remember my last assignment before Thanksgiving break required me to read eight chapters on Monday for a test on Friday. On the day of my exam, I was overwhelmed with thinking I hadn't studied enough due to the time I took crying and trying to manage the stressors in my home life. Before the test, the instructor announced coldly, "You have to pass with at least a 79% C. If you make 78% D, (which is failing), you will be dismissed from the class." By the grace of God, I made exactly a 79% C on my test, which meant I was able to continue to the next nursing class. My confidence was renewed as I felt I was still on the right track.

However, my renewed confidence was short-lived. During the last month of nursing school, my faith had become so shaken, I was full of anxiety. I had dropped to 100 pounds from the stress and lack of eating and sleeping. I took my pharmacology exam, which I had two chances to take to pass the first semester of nursing school. I failed it the first time and became hurt and emotionally overwhelmed. The night before I was to retake it the second time, I prayed and asked God to show favor over me to pass. I wanted so badly to stay in the program, to finish the race God had allowed me to run. I thanked Him in advance for victory.

On the morning of my pharmacology exam, I was panicked to find that my car wouldn't start and yelled, "Oh, God, not another setback!" After asking my husband to rush home so that I could use his car, I anxiously awaited his arrival. As I watched the hands on the clock get closer and closer to 8:00 am, my hands began trembling. I thought, 'Lord, what is going on? I've worked so hard during this whole semester. What are you saying to me?' My husband arrived at 7:30 a.m. and I made it to the school with only ten minutes to spare before class started. This meant I had no time to do a quick study. I went into class saying, "Not my will, but thine will be done." Sadly, to say I failed the second time also, and was dismissed from the nursing program.

What did all of this mean? I lost total confidence in myself after feeling let down by my failures and setbacks during nursing school. It took time for me to realize that my disappointment in self was due to me doing everything in *my* power. I was trying to be the perfect student by obsessing over my studying, staying up late, and worrying over things. I just wanted to be successful at a goal I'd set for myself and what I thought God wanted for me too. I was so depressed because instead of accepting God's will, I was wallowing in the failure and unfulfillment of my own will. I saw making the Dean's List, being inducted into an honor society, and being admitted to nursing school with a glimpse of a vision as God's validation that I was going to be successful at becoming a nurse. Ephesians 5:17 says, "Therefore do not be foolish, but understand what the will of the Lord is." Ultimately, God was only showing me that I would get into the program, but it was never revealed that I would complete it.

By learning to accept God's will over my own, and asking for forgiveness of not seeking wise counseling, I have been able to overcome my feelings of depression and anxiety surrounding this experience. I was also able to truly understand the humility of Jesus in Luke 22:42 when saying, 'Father, if it is Your will, take this cup away from Me; nevertheless, not My will, but Yours, be done (NKJV)."

Encouraged to Empower

We all live in a sometimes overwhelming, unpredictable world and our dreams can be that way too. When you have a dream and go after it, sometimes you don't always get it right but that's okay. Stay true to your thoughts and don't second guess yourself because most likely the first thought is the best answer.

With that being said, I hope these words of empowerment will help you on your journey.

1. **Before you decide to move in your own will**, know that God has a purpose for you even when it's not the one you would like to have. Try sitting at Jesus' feet for at least two to three minutes in silence and then begin to share with God your concerns. Wait to hear a response and know that sometimes it may not come in that moment, but throughout the day. It may even come as a simple phone call, an inspirational song or through a co-worker.

Do you have faith? Do you trust him?

_____

_____

2. **Do not be too hard on yourself.** Embrace your accomplishments by journaling your wins.

   What are you really afraid of?

   _____

   _____

3. **Lastly, find your inner peace.** You can do this by scheduling some _me_ time, meditate to relaxing music, or have a cup of coffee outside reading your favorite book.

   If not now, then when?

   _____

   _____

Be encouraged to not let your perfectionist tendencies, deficiencies or setbacks get in the way of your confidence. Things may get out of hand in your mind, but you can prevent them from getting the best of you. We are not to sabotage ourselves, nor are we expected to always be superb. We also have to be careful not to allow anxiety overwhelm us on any level because of our failures, which are really lessons. God didn't call us to be perfect. He loves us so much that He said His grace is enough for us, that his power is made perfect in us (2 Corinthians 12:9, ICB).

Pray with Me

Precious Father, You are so worthy to be praised. Thank you for being the merciful God that you are by keeping me in the center of your will. Not only that, but thank you for ordering my steps day by day. Thank you for giving me a peace of mind as I continue to walk with you on this journey. Thank you for reminding me that I don't have to be perfect because my confidence comes from you, through your Holy word.

The lost coin of confidence has now been found.
Let us rejoice in the name of Jesus. Amen.

~About Sharifa~

Sharifa Stirgus is a servant, devoted wife, prayer intercessor, and proud mother of two whom she loves to spend time with.

She is the author of *Letters to God With Gratitude:31 Days of Giving Thanks Devotional Journal* and co-author of the Anthology tilted, *I Am Who God Says I Am: Living My Life on Purpose.* She has obtained three Certificates of Completion for *The Teacher I Want to Be, How to Study the Bible and How to Teach the Bible.*

A graduate of UA-Pulaski Technical College, she earned an Associates of Science and certificate of Pre-Health Care Studies. She is currently a Certified Phlebotomist of 22 years.

She has a passion for the broken hearted and is a member of the Embrace Ministries Team, where she serves as a leader in the ministry of inspiring women.

Sharifa can be contacted at

authorsharifastirgus@gmail.com.

Two Questions

"You can make many plans, but the LORD's purpose will prevail."
~Proverbs 19:21, NLT~

Have you ever been presented the opportunity to be a part of something that had the potential to enhance you in some way? Sure you have! You prayed about it, then you said "Yes" without necessarily waiting for God's response. Or maybe you said "Yes", dismissing the slight nagging feeling inside because of the person's position or title. I don't think I need to tell you you're not alone. How many times have we said "Yes" to opportunities that were good ideas, but not necessarily God's idea for us? When we're longing to belong, wanting to fit in, feeling like we're missing out, there's a tendency to stray away from the direction or path God has laid out for us. When I found myself in such a situation recently, two questions were asked of me that rendered me speechless, "Did you ask God? What did he say?"

Before I share my response, I need to go back to the year 2018. Admittedly, I've had a tendency to say *yes* to groups, organizations, church plant efforts, and outreach efforts without really consulting God because I believed in the vision. I love helping. I love giving back and serving. I love helping people reach their goals. For the most part, I fulfilled my assigned responsibilities and moved on. But things began to hit a little bit differently in late 2018. I gave two people a *yes* that I didn't consult God about. I believed in the vision shared and didn't mind sharing my time, gifts, and talents. I should also add these *yes's* came at a time when I was hoping to find where I belonged. I wanted to be a part of something with longevity, meaning, and impact.

Unfortunately, after saying *yes* and putting in work for several months, my spirit became troubled. Like a lot of back and forth in my mind about what didn't seem right, wasn't adding up, or wasn't organized properly. For anyone who personally knows me, disorganization is one of my pet peeves. Knowing this of myself, I prayed that I wasn't being too picky or allowing preferences to get in the way. I've had to learn over time not to be too picky about certain things.

I reached out to someone I knew and trusted about one of the 'projects' and got an earful as we often say. The things that troubled me were confirmed. Then it became a matter of 'How do I get out of this?' HEREIN lies a problem. It's so easy to say "Yes", but mannn....when you have to turn around and say "No" – and not necessarily because of something they did, but simply because you didn't ask God's permission in the first place – that's not a good feeling. Now, God is indeed merciful, but sometimes we get ourselves in situations that we also have to get ourselves out of. He'll protect us, but the hard part will fall on us.

That was the first project. Now, for the second project. This was the most perplexing one because of who was involved, my genuine admiration for the leader, because of my own excitedness in the beginning and work put in, not to mention promises made and words given. Whew Jesus! I'm being a bit careful with my words, but when I say my spirit became uneasy, it was not letting me rest. Again, I checked myself on some things making sure "I" wasn't getting in the way or being too picky. But something happened that caused a very uneasy feeling in my spirit, and soon became something I just couldn't shake.

It wasn't anything against me, but another group of people, whom I'd just met on a Sunday, and was introduced as a part of a new project. There was some kind of phone exchange late in the evening, and the leader decided it was best to walk away. One day they're celebrating, the next, it's over. Wait! What?!? I was floored and heartbroken for those involved. Much akin to a marriage breakup, then begins the process of who keeps what, who's going with who, etc. I had no parts of that, but now it's another matter of how do I get out of something I was so committed to being a part of?

Two decisions to make at the same time. To myself I thought, 'This is not going to be good'. I stalled as long as I could. I prayed and I waited for some kind of re-direction. Then ONE day... I can't remember the exact words, nor can I find the post, but I remember coming across a Facebook meme that said something to the effect of, "It's a dangerous thing to stay in a place you're not meant to be in." Well now! That one meme convicted my heart so, I knew I couldn't delay any longer. I reached out and shared I could no longer be a part of either project. One accepted it with thanks and well wishes. The other, as I'd expected – there was a certain vibe afterwards.

Two years later, I found myself in yet another *project* situation where I ignored the nagging feeling that this wasn't the project for me, but because of the person, because of our brief, yet influential history, and because it was a good idea, I said, "Yes." I'm guessing not even two months in, there were raised eyebrows thinking, 'Hmm?!?' I'm not a confrontational person so I didn't say anything. It was a little thing said at first that I had first-hand knowledge of and knew wasn't completely true. Time passes and I'm seeing a different persona coming through. *Again*, I had to check myself because I know me. I don't take too kindly to how people say certain things. Over time, I've had to learn how not to take some things so personal. I may not say anything, but it becomes a mental note for sure. I still stayed quiet and obedient. But then we were asked to share something on social media that I was not in agreement with because it seemed to be against the true context of the passage.

To myself I'm thinking, 'I'm too deep in the project, one more payment to make'. Spirit uneasy again. 'No one to talk to. Seeing things, but can't really speak on it. Not my place to expose.' Constant thoughts going through my mind. I couldn't hold it in any longer, so finally I reached out to an Apostle that I've grown to trust over the last two years. I shared first because I just needed to get some things off my chest, trying to make sense of it all. She listened, made a few remarks, but before she fully explained the situation, she asked two questions in the moment that I will never forget, "Did you ask God first, and what did he say?"

She didn't want an explanation out of defense, just a simple *yes* or *no*. I was speechless, as she repeated, "It's a simple *yes* or *no*." And probably in a child-like voice, I responded, "No." I knew before we spoke I needed to remove myself, but man, not again! After further conversing, she said, "You know what you need to do. Be obedient!" So I handled the last payment and walked away.

None of these were easy decisions to make, and God could've orchestrated things in such a way that I didn't have to make a decision. However, if we never learn from our mistakes, we continue the same bad decision-making expecting a way out as opposed to accepting the responsibility. Our path has already been laid out for us if we would just seek God and not get caught up in titles, opportunities, or relationships. So the next time you're approached with something, no matter how simple or harmless it seems, remember the questions, "Did you ask God, and what did He say?"

Encouraged to Empower

It's easy to get caught up in what's trending, what all the 'experts' say you should be doing and what works. It's easy to get caught up with first impressions, but I leave you with these three things that I've learned along the way.

1. **Fast/Pray:** Corporate fast/prayer is good, but sometimes you need to do your own, and get away from the standard way of fasting. Yes, you can fast from food, but is that really the thing distracting you from being at one with God? Food is definitely a distraction for me, but it may not be for you. For you it may be social media, TV, your phone, shopping, or hanging with friends. What's the thing you go to first before going to God when you're frustrated, sad, upset, or feeling some type of way? Fast from that. One thing I've also found very beneficial is to make a list of what you're seeking direction, instruction, or clarity on. Be intentional and direct about what you need help with.

When did you last fast/pray? What are some things other than food that you can fast from? When will you fast/pray again?

_____

_____

_____

2. **Listen:** After you fast and pray, listen for the voice of God. Don't move until you hear. Now I don't necessarily mean that physically, but if you intended to only fast for one day, three days, or seven, but you have yet to hear God speak to your requests, continue to fast. Listen like you've never listened before, meaning maybe he spoke to you through a sermon one time. However, as you level up, he may speak to you a different way. Never get too comfortable with one way of listening.

What are some distractions to be mindful of in your environment? What are the different ways you believe God has spoken to you?

_____

_____

_____

_____

_____

3. **What's your why and what:** Sharifa mentioned this in her story, but I want to reiterate it here. Before you say _yes_ again, consider your why. Why do you want to be part of a specific something? Why do you feel it's a good idea for you? What are you hoping to gain? Lastly, examine your responses. Did they start with "I feel" or "I think"? If so, that's the first clue that maybe you're following your own direction versus God's direction.

Based on your current circumstance, what's your why for wanting to connect to someone (person

or organization)? What do you hope to gain from the connection or collaboration?

_____

_____

_____

_____

_____

These steps have been helpful in the sense that I've been challenged to be still before making a decision. I've been challenged to discern if the direction I'm being led in has been ordained or approved by God. These steps have also put me in a better position for God to trust me with greater – not necessarily in material things, but more so regarding assignments and responsibilities.

Pray with Me

Abba Father, Thank You for embracing me, for reminding me that I do have a place to which I belong and am well accepted. Thank you for your redemptive grace – saving me from situations, people, and even myself simply because I failed to listen. Thank you for your gracious mercy – for blessing me in spite of decisions made apart from your plan. Thank you for trusting me even when I've failed to trust you. May that which I've endured serve as a lesson and reminder that I am to seek first your kingdom and everything else will fall in place. Lord I trust you will not direct me the wrong way, and even when it doesn't make sense, I will listen because you've never failed.

The lost coin of direction has now been found.
Let us rejoice in the name of Jesus. Amen.

~About Kocysha~

Kocysha LaShaun is a long-time resident of Central Arkansas where she wrote her first book, *Humbled by His Grace* in 2013. Seven years later, she self-published the mini-book series, *See Self as God Sees.* She is the co-author/co-editor for the anthology titled, *I Am Who God Says I Am: Living My Life On Purpose*, and a co-author in the anthology, *Courage 2 Serve* presented by Embrace Ministries 365. Kocysha, aka Minister Koko, currently serves on the Embrace team helping lead prayer and study classes.

In early 2020, Kocysha completed additional coaching certifications through Transformation Academy to lend to her calling as a Spiritual Mindset Coach. As the founder of Be Accelerated into Purpose, LLC, and Humbled by His Grace Ministries, Kocysha's mission is simply to remind others of the love and grace of God so they can fully walk in their purpose.

For more info, please visit www.kocyshalashaun.com.

ABOUT THE AUTHORS

Each author is influential and has passion with the heart of God to inspire and help women who struggle with identity, validation crisis, manipulation, and more. If you've been challenged in similar areas, we hope you've been encouraged and empowered to find your missing piece in God himself through the tips shared. May you, too, find your reason to rejoice with friends and family!

We'd love to stay connected. Check us out at www.TheLostCoinAP.com to see what happens next.

Also, please leave us a review on Amazon.

Blessings from the

Ladies of The Lost Coin Anthology Project!

Made in the USA
Columbia, SC
09 February 2021